BEADS

written by
Judy Ann Sadler

illustrated by Marilyn Mets

KIDS CAN PRESS LTD.

Toronto

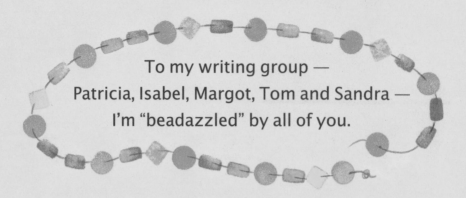

To my writing group —
Patricia, Isabel, Margot, Tom and Sandra —
I'm "beadazzled" by all of you.

Canadian Cataloguing in Publication Data

Sadler, Judy Ann, 1959-
    Beads

(Kids can easy crafts)
Issued also in French under title Les perles.
ISBN 1-55074-182-9

1. Beads — Juvenile literature. 2. Beadwork — Juvenile literature.
3. Jewelry making — Juvenile literature. I. Mets, Marilyn. II. Title.
III. Series.

T1860.S3 1993   j746.5   C93-095081-X

Kids Can Press Ltd.   Edited by Laurie Wark
29 Birch Avenue   Designed by Nancy Ruth Jackson
Toronto, Ontario, Canada   Printed and bound in Hong Kong
M4V 1E2
94 0 9 8 7 6 5 4 3 2 1

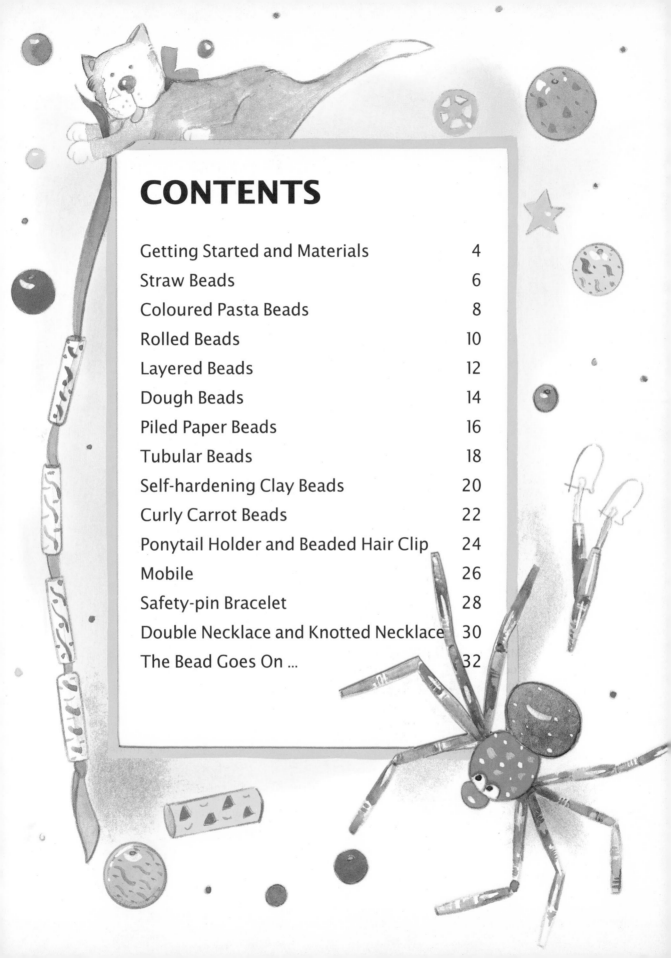

CONTENTS

GETTING STARTED

What can be any shape, size or colour, plain or fancy, heavy or light and can be hung up, strung up, rolled up or cut up? Give up? Beads! Baskets and bags of beads. Make them from paper, pasta, dough and clay. Hang them from doorknobs and zippers or glue them onto boxes, hats and shoes. Make mobiles, jewellery, toys and more. You will find many of the things you need for beadmaking around your home. Be sure to keep your supplies and small beads away from your younger brother or sister. Now gather the materials you see on these pages, decide what to make first and bead it!

Materials and Helpful Hints

paper Newspaper, colour comics, used wrapping paper, construction paper and shiny magazine and catalogue pages can all be used for making beads.

making holes Toothpicks, bamboo skewers, knitting needles and plastic drinking straws can be used to make holes in your beads. They are also helpful for holding beads as you paint them.

accessories If you would like to be able to open and close a necklace or bracelet, tie a paper clip onto each end of the string and use them as fasteners. You can reuse fasteners from old or broken necklaces, earrings, brooches and bracelets, too. Check craft and jewellery supply stores for all kinds of jewellery findings.

coatings Use acrylic craft paint, acrylic varnish, glossy Podgy or a similar product to put a protective, shiny, water-resistant finish on your beads. These products are non-toxic, and they clean up with soap and water.

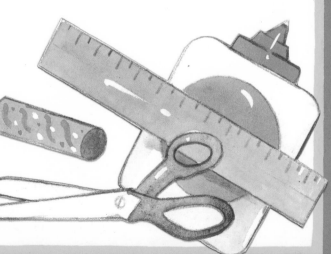

other stuff You will also need good-quality, clear-drying, non-toxic white glue, paintbrushes, scissors and a ruler. Keep a wet cloth handy to wipe glue off your fingers.

stringing beads Use string, yarn, embroidery thread, fishing line, dental floss, invisible nylon thread, leather cord, plastic lace, ribbon or elastic thread for stringing your beads. To make a secure knot, tie the right string over the left string and then the left string over the right string.

STRAW BEADS

THINGS YOU NEED:

ruler
pencil
scissors
colour comics or used wrapping
  paper
white glue
drinking straws

1 Measure, mark and cut strips of paper 5 cm (2 inches) wide and one and a half times the length of your straw.

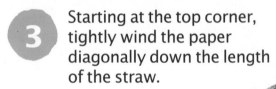

2 Spread a thin coating of glue on one side of a strip of paper. Make sure the glue goes right to the edges.

3 Starting at the top corner, tightly wind the paper diagonally down the length of the straw.

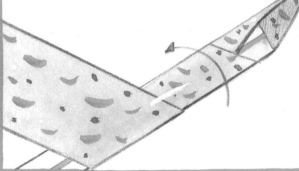

4 Cut off the paper points at each end of the straw.

5 Cut the straw into beads, any size you like. They will go flying as you cut, so watch out! If there are any loose paper edges on your beads, glue them down.

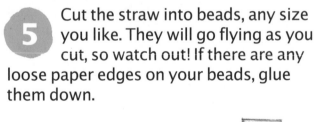

Fun ideas to try

◆ Before you cut your straw beads, coat them with acrylic varnish or Podgy.

◆ Instead of stringing all the beads through the holes, use a needle to poke holes through the sides of the beads so that they will hang the other way.

◆ Use plain strips of paper and decorate them with crayons, markers or sparkles before you cut them into beads.

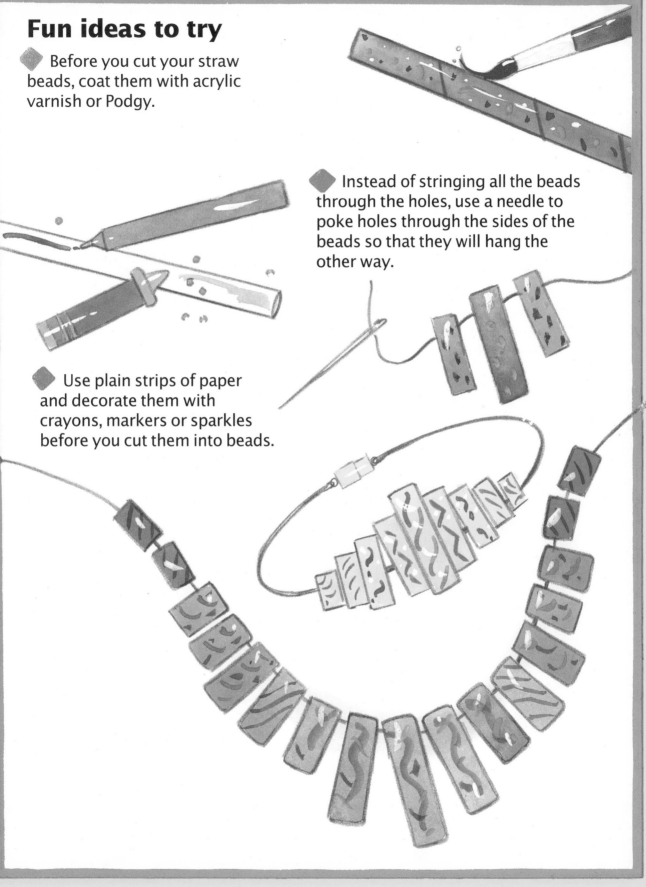

COLOURED PASTA BEADS

THINGS YOU NEED:

newspaper
plastic bag
measuring cup and spoons
liquid food colour
elbow macaroni
spoon
waxed paper

1 Spread a double thickness of newspaper over your work space.

2 Make sure your plastic bag does not have a hole in it. Pour 5 mL (1 teaspoon) of food colour into the plastic bag.

3 Add 125 mL (½ cup) of macaroni to the bag. Twist and hold the bag closed.

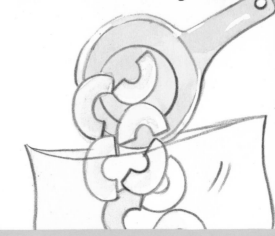

4 Cover the pieces of macaroni with food colour by shaking them around in the bag.

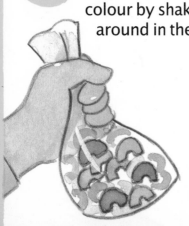

5 Empty the coloured macaroni onto the newspaper. Spread it around with a spoon. The newspaper helps to soak up the extra liquid.

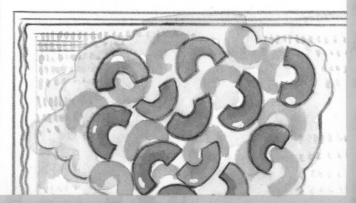

6 Before the macaroni dries and sticks to the newspaper, slide it onto a sheet of waxed paper. Spread it around with the spoon so that the pieces are not touching.

7 Let the pieces dry for about half an hour. String them and see the neat squiggly pattern they make. This macaroni is not for eating. Also, be careful not to get the pasta wet, or the colour may run.

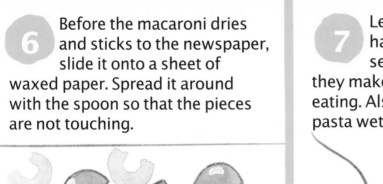

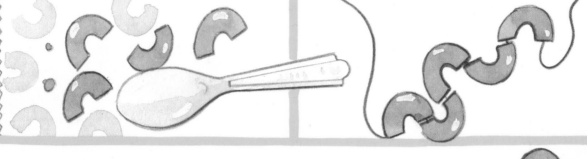

Fun ideas to try

◆ Any pasta with a hole can be used. Try wagon wheels, rigatoni and macaroni in different sizes.

◆ For an interesting crackled look, add a little water to the food colour in the bag. Drain the pasta in a colander before drying it on newspaper and waxed paper.

◆ Mix the liquid food colours to create new colours for your pasta beads.

ROLLED BEADS

THINGS YOU NEED:

sheet of paper
pencil
ruler
scissors
white glue
lightweight cardboard
shiny, colourful magazine or
   catalogue pages
round toothpicks

1 Fold the sheet of paper in half. Make a dot on the folded edge 15 cm (6 inches) up from the bottom. Make another dot 1.5 cm ($^5/_8$ inch) from the fold along the bottom edge. Join these dots with a ruler.

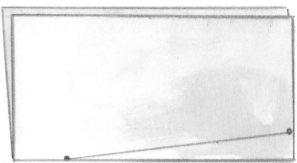

2 Cut along this line. Open the paper and glue it onto a piece of lightweight cardboard. Cut it out. This is your pattern.

3 Use your cardboard pattern to trace triangles onto the catalogue or magazine pages, as shown.

4 Cut out the triangles. You will need about 25 triangles to make a necklace. Cut out extras so that you can make other things, too.

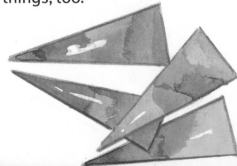

5 To make the beads, wind the wide end of the triangle around a toothpick. Guide the paper with one hand as you roll, so that the point of the triangle ends up in the middle of the bead.

6 Spread some glue on the last 3 cm (1 inch) of the triangle and smooth it down flat. Hold it in place for a moment as the glue dries.

7 Carefully take the bead off the toothpick and wind on another one.

Fun ideas to try

For extra thick and glossy beads, cut triangles from magazine or catalogue covers.

Try cutting longer, wider or narrower triangles and experiment with different shapes, too.

Make rolled beads out of colour comics or used wrapping paper. Finish these beads with acrylic varnish or Podgy while they are still on the toothpicks. Stick them into a potato, sponge or Plasticine to dry.

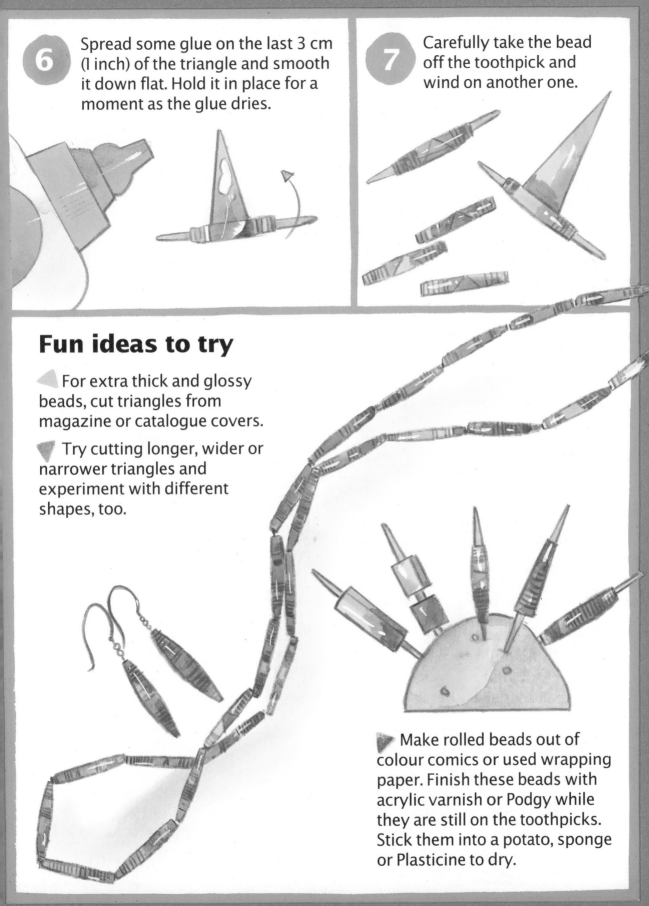

LAYERED BEADS

THINGS YOU NEED:

pencil
ruler
construction paper
scissors
drinking straws or toothpicks
white glue
paintbrush
acrylic varnish or Podgy

1 Cut three different colours of construction paper into long strips. Cut some strips 3 cm (1 inch) wide, some 2 cm (3/4 inches) wide and others 1 cm (1/2 inch) wide.

2 Cut these strips into pieces about 8 cm (3 inches) long.

3 Roll a wide piece of paper onto a straw or toothpick. Keep the sides even. Spread a bit of glue on the last 3 cm (1 inch) and smooth the edges down flat. Hold the paper for a moment while the glue dries.

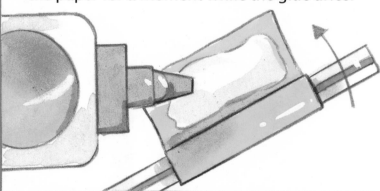

4 Dab a bit of glue in the centre of the rolled paper on your straw.

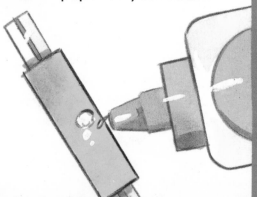

5 Take a medium-width piece of paper and centre it on the wide piece on your straw. Roll it, glue the last 3 cm (1 inch) and hold it for a moment as the glue dries.

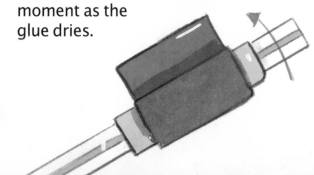

6 Dab a bit of glue in the centre of the bead. Roll and glue a narrow piece of paper on top, so that you now have three layers.

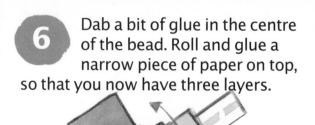

7 While the bead is still on the straw, coat it with acrylic varnish or Podgy. When it is dry, slide the bead off.

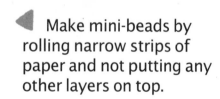

Fun ideas to try

▲ Make large beads by using longer, wider strips of construction paper and layering narrower ones on top.

◀ Make mini-beads by rolling narrow strips of paper and not putting any other layers on top.

▶ Roll ribbon or fabric strips onto a straw.

DOUGH BEADS

THINGS YOU NEED:

mixing bowl
fork
measuring cups
flour
salt
water
liquid food colour
plastic bags
cookie cutters
waxed paper or foil-lined cookie sheet
drinking straw, pencil or toothpick
paintbrush
acrylic varnish or Podgy

1 In a mixing bowl, stir together 250 mL (1 cup) of flour and 50 mL (¼ cup) of salt. Add enough water to hold the dough together, about 125 mL (½ cup).

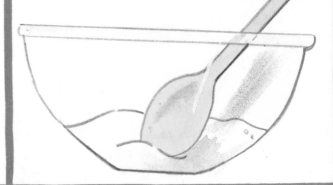

2 Mix the dough with your hands. If it does not hold together, add a little more water. If it is sticky, add a little flour. The dough is just right when it does not stick to your hands.

3 Divide the dough into lumps. Add a few drops of food colour to each lump and work them in until you have a solid colour. For a marbled look, do not work the colour in too much. (Put the dough you are not using into plastic bags, so that it does not dry out. If your dough gets a little dry, work in a few drops of water.)

4 Make beads by pulling off some dough and rolling it between your palms. Roll little beads between your thumb and index finger.

5 You can also use cookie cutters on this dough. Pat some dough flat on waxed paper and press a cookie cutter into it.

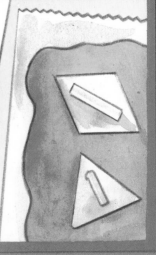

6 Make holes in your beads with a straw, a pencil or a toothpick. If you are going to bake your beads, make a large hole. The heat will puff up the beads and cause a small hole to close.

7 Place your beads in a warm, dry place to air-dry for a few days. Or put the beads on a foil-lined cookie sheet and ask an adult to bake them in the oven at 120°C (250°F) for two to four hours. When the beads are dry, you may want to coat them with acrylic varnish or Podgy.

Fun ideas to try

- Form the dough into other shapes, such as cubes, cylinders and spirals.

- Press designs into your beads using a fork or a toothpick.

- Mix together different-coloured pieces of dough to make multi-coloured beads.

- Paint your dough beads instead of using food colour.

PILED PAPER BEADS

THINGS YOU NEED:

pencil
construction paper
small bottle lid
scissors
hole punch
white glue

heavy book
sandpaper
paintbrush
acrylic varnish
or Podgy

1 Trace circles onto two or three different colours of construction paper using a small bottle lid as the pattern.

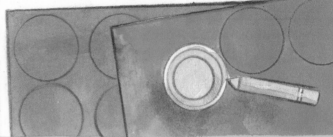

2 Cut out the circles. Depending on how thick you would like your bead to be, you will need between 20 and 40 circles.

3 Punch a hole in one of the circles. Use this hole as a guide for punching holes in the other circles.

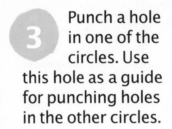

4 Spread a thin layer of glue on each circle as you pile one on top of the other. Try to match up the holes and edges of each circle. Arrange the circles in layers of colour, so that they make stripes.

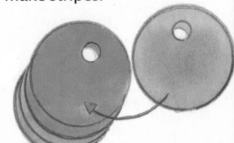

5 Place a heavy book on your bead and let the glue dry overnight.

6 Sand the edges to make them smooth. Paint your piled paper bead with acrylic varnish or Podgy.

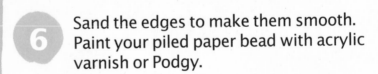

Fun ideas to try

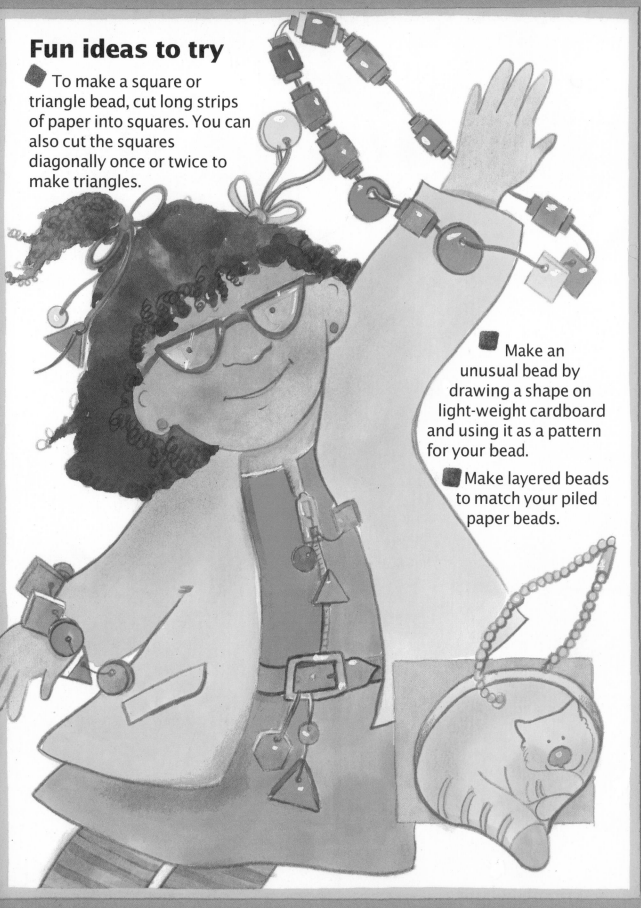

To make a square or triangle bead, cut long strips of paper into squares. You can also cut the squares diagonally once or twice to make triangles.

Make an unusual bead by drawing a shape on light-weight cardboard and using it as a pattern for your bead.

Make layered beads to match your piled paper beads.

TUBULAR BEADS

THINGS YOU NEED:

ruler
pencil
newspaper
Popsicle stick
measuring spoon
white glue
water

aluminum pie plate
  or old bowl
drinking straws
paintbrush
acrylic craft paint
acrylic varnish or
  Podgy

1 Use a ruler to measure and tear strips of newspaper 3 cm x 20 cm (1 inch x 8 inches).

2 Use the Popsicle stick to stir together 10 mL (2 teaspoons) of glue with 10 mL (2 teaspoons) of water in the pie plate.

3 Pull a newspaper strip through the glue mixture. (Both sides of the strip do not need to get wet.) Run it through your index and middle fingers to get rid of any extra glue.

4 Roll the strip onto a straw, keeping the edges even. If the end pops up, hold it down for a moment or put a little extra glue under it.

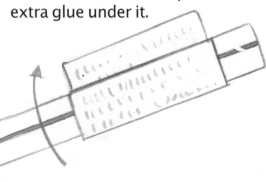

5 Wind three or four beads onto each straw. Rest the straws across a cup or bowl and let the beads dry overnight.

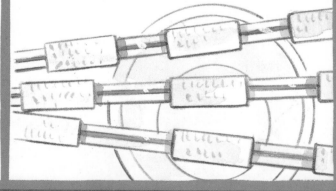

6 Paint the beads while they are still on the straws. Begin by painting each bead a solid colour and letting it dry. Then add dots, lines and splotches with other colours. Let the paint dry.

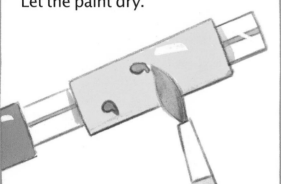

7 Coat your beads with acrylic varnish or Podgy. They should slide off the straws easily when they are completely dry. Pull off any bits of dry paint from around the edges of the beads.

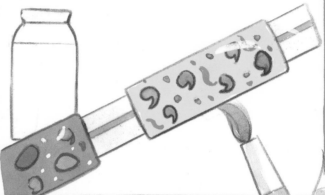

Fun ideas to try

● Give your beads a marbled look by gently mixing some wet paint colours on the beads.

● Make tubular beads in different widths.

● Glue some sparkles onto the beads before you give them a final clear coating.

SELF-HARDENING CLAY BEADS

THINGS YOU NEED:

self-hardening clay from a craft supply store
wet cloth
toothpicks, bamboo skewers or
    knitting needles
plate or waxed paper
paintbrush
acrylic craft paint

1 Pull off a small amount of clay. (Keep the rest of the clay covered in its plastic bag or container.)

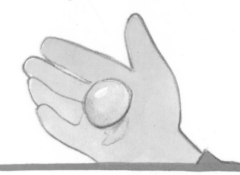

2 Roll the clay in your palms until it is round. This clay dries quickly. You may need to wet your hands with the cloth if the clay starts to crack.

3 Make lots of different-sized beads. Use a toothpick to poke holes in small beads and a knitting needle to make holes in large ones. If you get a bump on the end of the bead where the toothpick comes out, smooth it down.

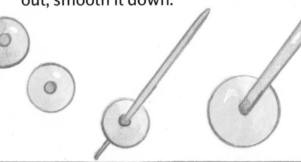

4 Place your beads on a plate or a sheet of waxed paper. Let them harden overnight. In the morning, you may need to turn over very large beads to help them finish drying.

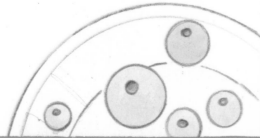

5 When the beads are hard and dry, decorate them with acrylic paint. Hold them on toothpicks, bamboo skewers or knitting needles as you paint, and set them across a bowl or cup to dry.

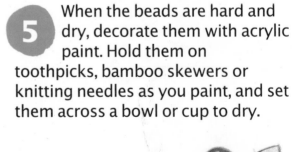

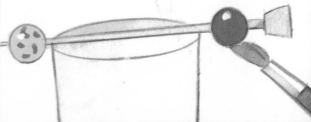

Fun ideas to try

Make hearts, stars, fish, dice, braids, spirals or any shape you like out of the clay. Be sure to poke holes in the beads so that you can string them.

Try making colourful beads out of oven-hardening modelling clay such as Fimo or Sculpey. Ask an adult to help you bake the beads following the instructions on the package.

CURLY CARROT BEADS

THINGS YOU NEED:

paring knife
cutting board
thick carrots
scissors
yarn
large needle

piece of corrugated
cardboard

1 Ask an adult to help you thinly slice a carrot. The slices should be about the thickness of a coin.

2 Cut a piece of yarn about 1 m (3 feet) long. Thread it through the needle.

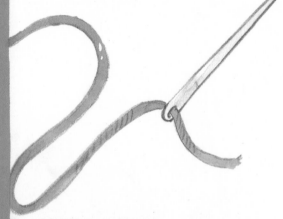

3 Place a slice of carrot on the piece of corrugated cardboard. Poke the needle into the centre of the carrot, pick it up and thread it onto the yarn.

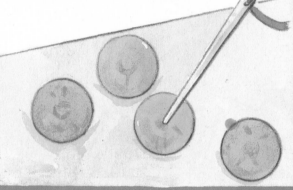

4 String all the carrots this way. Leave 3 cm (1 inch) of yarn between each slice.

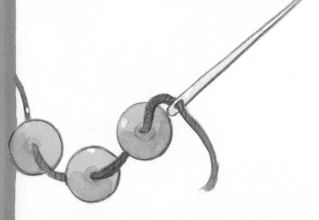

5 Hang the carrots from a kitchen chair or a doorknob. (Be careful when you close the door!)

6 Let the carrot slices hang overnight. In the morning, move the slices a little bit down the yarn so that they do not get stuck. It may take two days for them to dry.

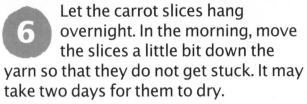

7 When the curly carrot beads are completely dry, take them off the yarn, or push them together, trim the yarn and knot your new necklace.

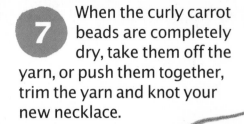

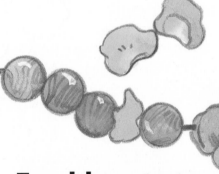

Fun ideas to try

▶ Make a necklace by stringing round wooden beads in between the curly carrot beads.

▲ For variety, cut small but thick carrot slices and dry them. Or cut large, thin slices into quarters and string them to let them dry.

PONYTAIL HOLDER

THINGS YOU NEED:

scissors
ribbon
beads

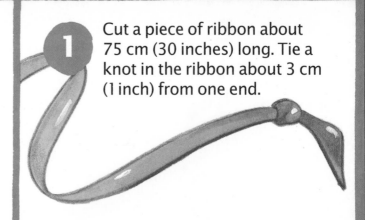

1 Cut a piece of ribbon about 75 cm (30 inches) long. Tie a knot in the ribbon about 3 cm (1 inch) from one end.

2 Thread on a variety of beads with large holes. Try straw beads, layered beads or any neat beads you have bought or collected. The first bead you thread on should not move past the knot on your ribbon. If it does, choose a bead with a smaller hole or make your knot larger.

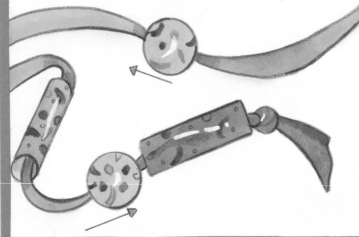

3 When you have filled up about 10 cm (4 inches) of the ribbon, thread matching beads onto the other end. When you have filled up 10 cm (4 inches) on that end, knot your ribbon.

4 Tie the decorated ribbon around your ponytail, or give it as a gift to a long-haired friend or relative.

BEADED HAIR CLIP

THINGS YOU NEED:

straw beads
scissors
ruler
white glue
hair clip
paintbrush
acrylic varnish or Podgy
narrow ribbon

1 Make straw beads and cut them into 1.5-cm (5/8-inch) lengths. You will need between 10 and 20 beads.

2 Spread lots of glue on the hair clip. Set the beads in the glue side by side, with no spaces in between.

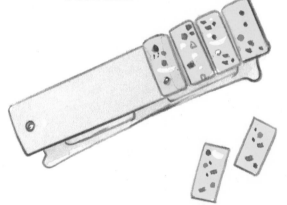

3 When the glue has started to dry, apply a coat of acrylic varnish or Podgy over the beads. Let it dry for a couple of hours.

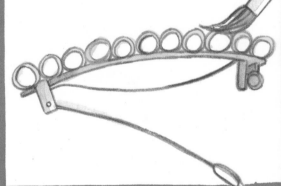

4 Cut two pieces of ribbon, each about 25 cm (10 inches) long. Poke them down through three or four of the centre beads and lightly glue them in place. Cut some of the leftover straw beads in half and tie them onto these ribbon ends.

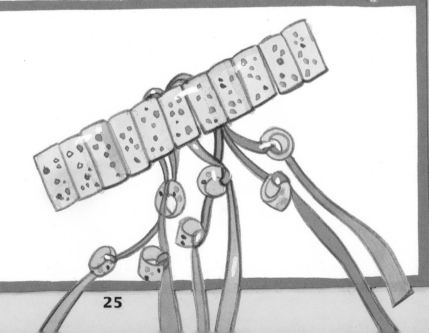

MOBILE

THINGS YOU NEED:

small bowl
pencil
corrugated or stiff cardboard
construction paper
scissors
hole punch
white glue
fishing line
ruler or measuring tape
an assortment of beads

1 Use the bowl to trace one circle on the cardboard and two on the construction paper. Cut them out.

2 Ask an adult to help you punch between 10 and 15 holes evenly around the edge of the cardboard circle.

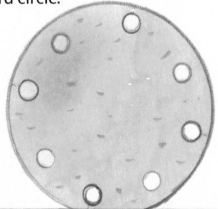

3 Glue one of the construction-paper circles onto one side of the cardboard circle and punch the holes. Glue the other construction-paper circle onto the other side and punch the holes.

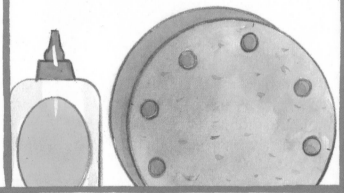

4 Cut a piece of fishing line 30 cm (12 inches) long. Thread on a round bead and tie a knot just above it. (The other beads will cover the knot.)

5 Decide on a pattern of beads and thread them on the line.

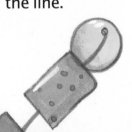

6 Poke the line through a hole in your cardboard circle and knot it tightly.

7 The next line you cut should be 33 cm (13 inches) long. Put the same type and number of beads on it. (You can change the colour and order of the beads.) Knot this line beside the first one.

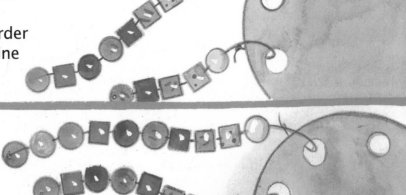

8 Keep adding 3 cm (1 inch) to the length of each line, and bead until you have hung one line from each hole in your cardboard circle.

9 Cut four more pieces of fishing line 60 cm (24 inches) each. Choose four holes about the same distance apart and ask someone to hold the mobile while you thread a line through each of the four holes. Bring all the ends together in the centre and knot them. Hang up your mobile and enjoy it!

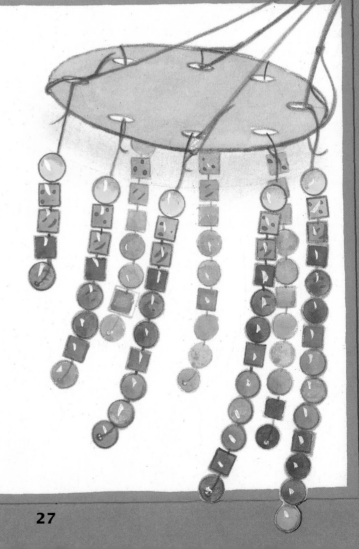

SAFETY-PIN BRACELET

THINGS YOU NEED:

about 20 rolled beads
about 20 medium-sized safety pins
scissors
60 cm (24 inches) of thin elastic thread
measuring tape
masking tape
about 40 straw beads cut into 0.5-cm (l/4-inch) pieces

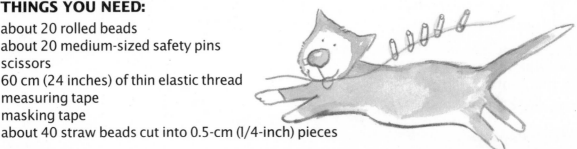

1 Make the rolled beads the right length to fit on your safety pins. Carefully open each pin, put on a rolled bead and close each pin.

2 Cut two pieces of elastic thread, each 30 cm (l2 inches) long. Tape the end of one piece of elastic to your work table.

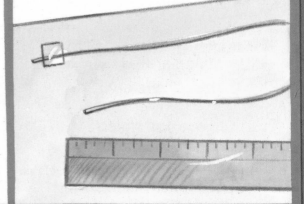

3 Poke the free end of this elastic through the round hole at the bottom of a beaded safety pin. Thread on a straw bead too.

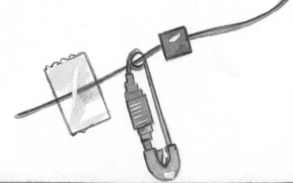

4 Now thread on another pin, but this time go through the hole at the top of the pin. Thread on another straw bead.

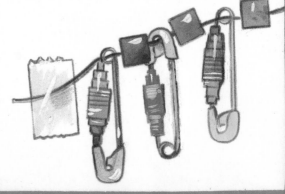

5 Continue this way: thread through the bottom of a pin, put on a straw bead, thread through the top of a pin and add another straw bead. Make sure that the rolled beads on the pins are all facing outwards.

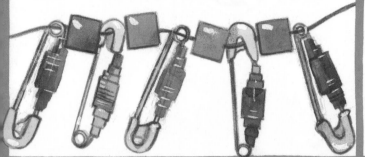

6 Measure your wrist and add 2 cm (³/₄ inch). This is how long your bracelet should be. As you reach this length, end with a pin threaded through the top, and a straw bead.

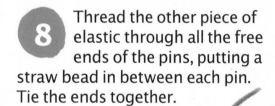

7 Remove the tape from the elastic thread and knot the ends together. To make this knot tight, tie the right thread over the left thread and then the left thread over the right thread.

8 Thread the other piece of elastic through all the free ends of the pins, putting a straw bead in between each pin. Tie the ends together.

Fun ideas to try

◆ Thread beaded safety pins onto a necklace. Let them hang down freely in the centre.

◆ Use straw or small dough beads on the pins, instead of the rolled ones. Or try this bracelet with store-bought beads.

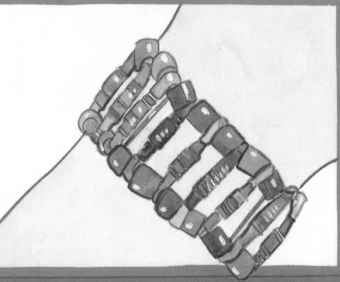

DOUBLE NECKLACE

THINGS YOU NEED:

scissors
some type of string
rolled, layered, straw or
    tubular beads

1 Cut a string twice as long as you would like your finished necklace to be. (Make sure it will be long enough to fit over your head.) Bring the ends together. Knot the looped end.

2 Thread a bead onto each string. Thread a third bead onto the doubled string.

3 Separate the strings again so that you can put another bead on each string. Keep stringing beads onto your necklace this way until you get near the end.

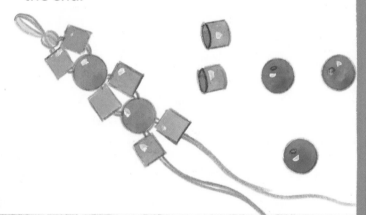

4 Finish your necklace by tying the ends of the string through the looped end.

KNOTTED NECKLACE

THINGS YOU NEED:

scissors
colourful string
measuring tape
an assortment of beads

1 Cut a piece of string 2 m (6¹/₂ feet) long. Cut it in half and bring all four ends together.

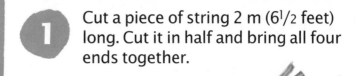

2 Knot the strings together 13 cm (5 inches) from the ends. (Make sure the loop will fit over your head.)

3 Thread beads onto each of the string ends and knot them in place.

Other jewellery ideas to try

Tie strings in between beads on a necklace and thread on more beads. Knot them in place.

Cut short strings and fold them in half. Make a knot near the looped end. Thread on beads and knot or glue them in place. Use the loop to hang your beaded strings from earrings.

Make a choker necklace with some favourite beads on a leather cord.

THE BEAD GOES ON . . .

Bead-toss Game Decorate a plastic or paper cup with construction paper. Poke a hole in the bottom of the cup. Push a piece of ribbon about 50 cm (20 inches) long through the hole from the bottom and knot it. Put a large bead on the other end and knot it in place. Toss the bead into the air and try to catch it in the cup.

Beady Spider Twist four pipe cleaners together in the middle and push them through a chunky bead with a large opening. Spread out the pipe cleaners to look like legs and dab a bit of glue on each one. Thread two rolled beads onto each leg. Glue on a small bead nose, roly eyes and another large bead for the body. Paint some interesting markings on your beady spider.

Bead It! Beads can be glued onto boxes, hair bands, sunglasses, ball-cap peaks, shoes, baskets and picture frames. String them on shoelaces, T-shirt fringes, key chains or your hair.

More Beads You can also make beads from other things, such as painted empty thread spools, buttons, metal washers and nuts, hollow grass and cardboard cut-outs.